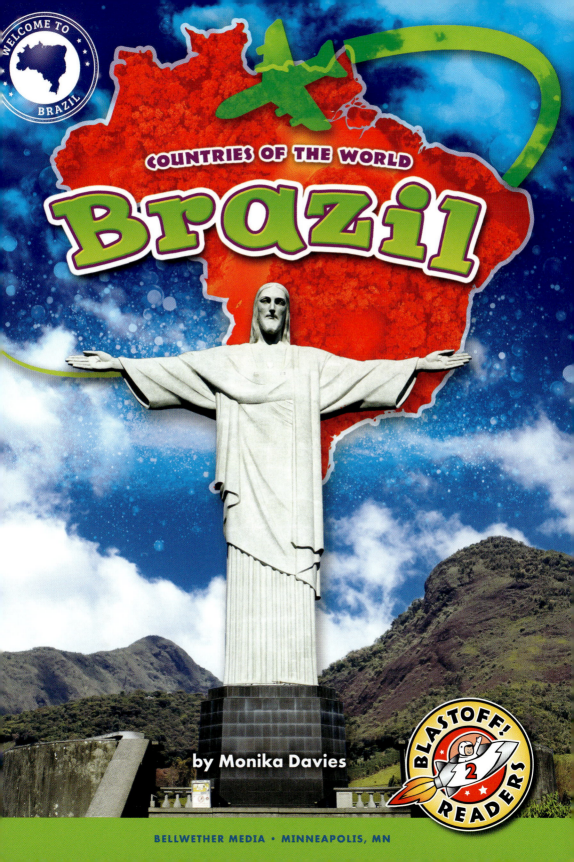

Blastoff! Readers are carefully developed by literacy experts to build reading stamina and move students toward fluency by combining standards-based content with developmentally appropriate text.

LEVELS

Level 1 provides the most support through repetition of high-frequency words, light text, predictable sentence patterns, and strong visual support.

Level 2 offers early readers a bit more challenge through varied sentences, increased text load, and text-supportive special features.

Level 3 advances early-fluent readers toward fluency through increased text load, less reliance on photos, advancing concepts, longer sentences, and more complex special features.

★ **Blastoff! Universe**

Reading Level

Grade K

Grades 1–3

Grade 4

This edition first published in 2023 by Bellwether Media, Inc.

No part of this publication may be reproduced in whole or in part without written permission of the publisher. For information regarding permission, write to Bellwether Media, Inc., Attention: Permissions Department, 6012 Blue Circle Drive, Minnetonka, MN 55343.

Library of Congress Cataloging-in-Publication Data

Names: Davies, Monika, author.
Title: Brazil / by Monika Davies.
Description: Minneapolis, MN : Bellwether Media, 2023. | Series: Blastoff! Readers: Countries of the world | Includes bibliographical references and index. | Audience: Ages 5-8 | Audience: Grades 2-3 | Summary: "Relevant images match informative text in this introduction to Brazil. Intended for students in kindergarten through third grade"– Provided by publisher.
Identifiers: LCCN 2022018178 (print) | LCCN 2022018179 (ebook) | ISBN 9781644877142 (library binding) | ISBN 9781648347603 (ebook)
Subjects: LCSH: Brazil–Juvenile literature.
Classification: LCC F2508.5 .D38 2023 (print) | LCC F2508.5 (ebook) | DDC 981–dc23/eng/20220414
LC record available at https://lccn.loc.gov/2022018178
LC ebook record available at https://lccn.loc.gov/2022018179

Text copyright © 2023 by Bellwether Media, Inc. BLASTOFF! READERS and associated logos are trademarks and/or registered trademarks of Bellwether Media, Inc.

Editor: Elizabeth Neuenfeldt   Designer: Gabriel Hilger
Printed in the United States of America, North Mankato, MN.

Table of Contents

All About Brazil	4
Land and Animals	6
Life in Brazil	12
Brazil Facts	20
Glossary	22
To Learn More	23
Index	24

All About Brazil

Brasília

Brazil is a nation in South America. It is the fifth-largest country in the world!

Brazil also has one of the world's largest **populations**. Its capital city is Brasília.

Land and Animals

The Amazon **Rain Forest** covers northern Brazil. It is the world's largest rain forest! It is warm year-round.

The Amazon River runs through this **tropical** forest.

Amazon Rain Forest

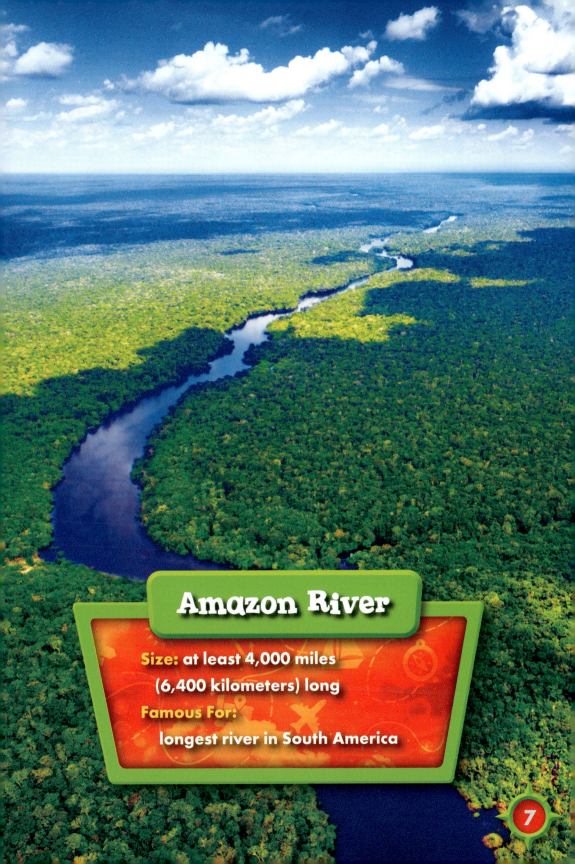

Amazon River

Size: at least 4,000 miles (6,400 kilometers) long

Famous For: longest river in South America

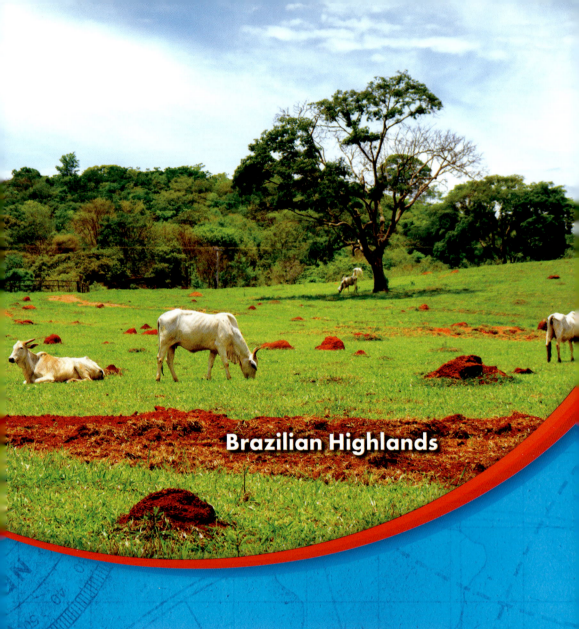

Brazilian Highlands

The Brazilian Highlands are in central Brazil. They are made of **grasslands**.

To the west is the Pantanal. It is the world's largest tropical **wetland**!

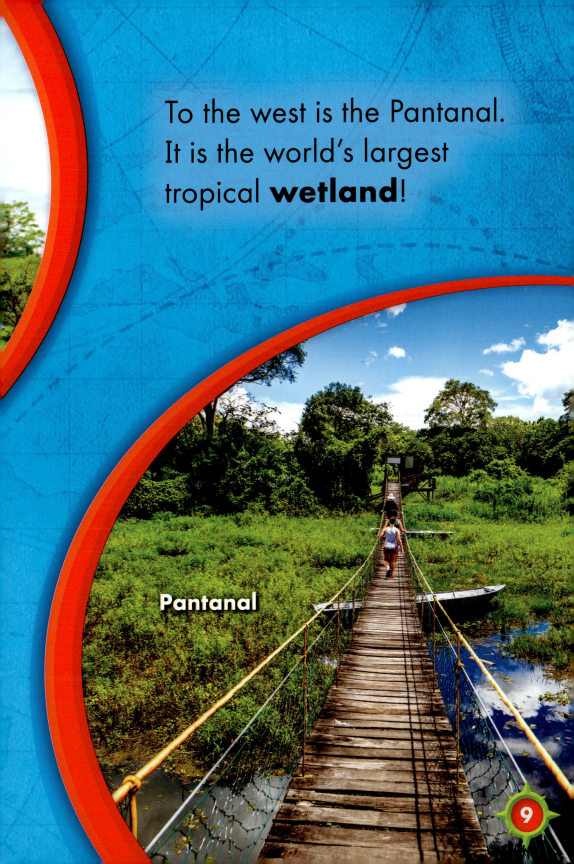

Pantanal

Many animals live in Brazil. Capybaras and macaws live in the Pantanal. Caimans hunt by the water.

capybaras

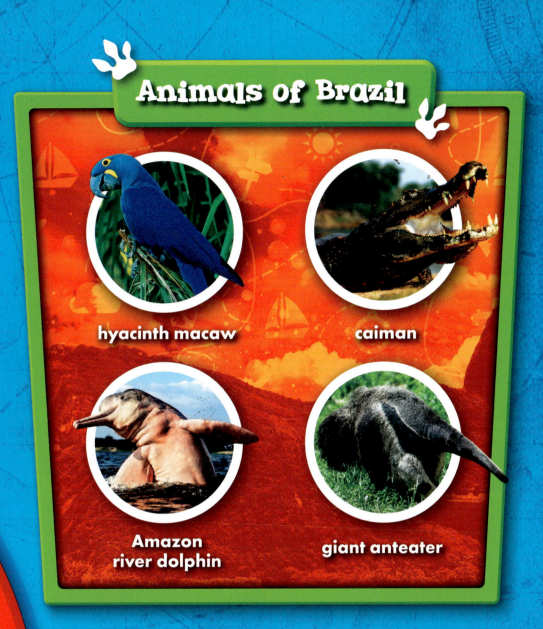

Dolphins swim in the Amazon River. Anteaters walk through the Brazilian Highlands.

Life in Brazil

Brazilians call this country home. They speak Portuguese. Many are **Catholics**.

Most Brazilians live in cities such as São Paulo.

Catholic church

Many Brazilian families enjoy spending time outside. They have picnics at parks and beaches.

Soccer is Brazil's favorite sport. Almost everyone plays it! Volleyball is also popular.

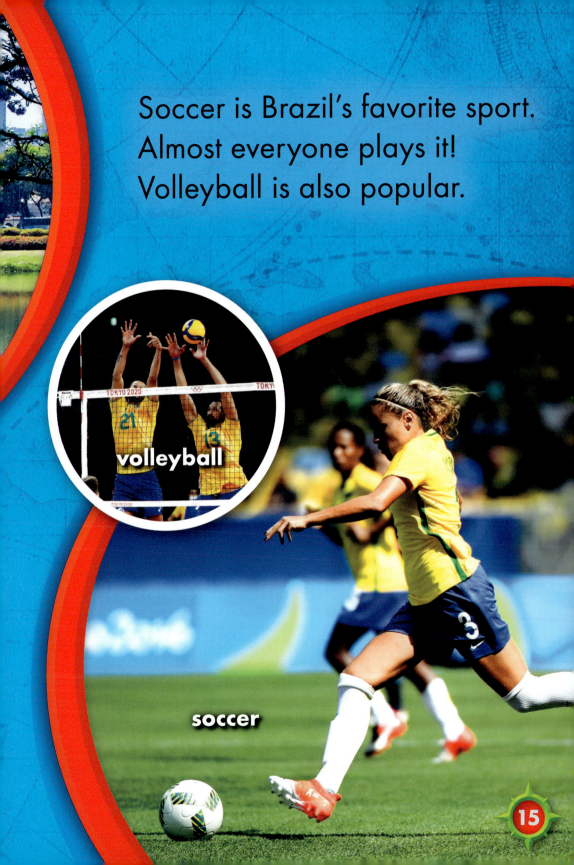

volleyball

soccer

People often eat *feijoada* on Wednesdays and Saturdays. It is a black bean stew.

Brazilian Foods

feijoada

quindim

brigadeiros

Many also love eating *quindim*.
It is a sweet **custard**.
Brigadeiros are another sweet treat.

Every year, Brazilians **celebrate** *Carnaval*. It happens before **Lent**. People dance and have huge parades.

Carnaval

Brazil's national holiday is on September 7. People watch fireworks. Holidays bring Brazilians together!

Brazil Facts

Size:
3,287,957 square miles
(8,515,770 square kilometers)

Population:
217,240,060 (2022)

National Holiday:
Independence Day (September 7)

Main Language:
Portuguese

Capital City:
Brasília

Famous Face

Name: Neymar da Silva Santos Júnior

Famous For: a professional soccer player

Religions

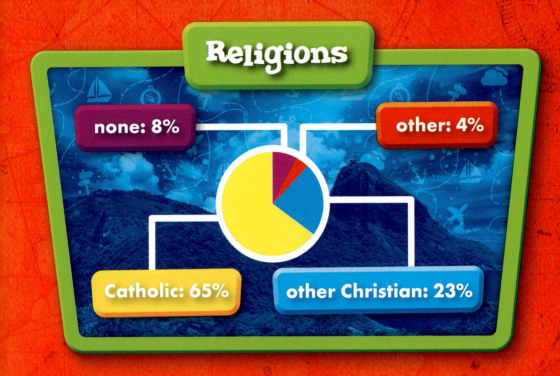

- none: 8%
- other: 4%
- Catholic: 65%
- other Christian: 23%

Top Landmarks

Christ the Redeemer

Iguaçu Falls

Sugar Loaf Mountain

Glossary

Catholics—people belonging or relating to the Christian church that is led by the pope

celebrate—to do something special or fun for an event, occasion, or holiday

custard—a kind of sweet food that is made with eggs and milk

grasslands—lands covered with grasses and other soft plants with few bushes or trees

Lent—a period of 40 days when Christians prepare for Easter

populations—total numbers of people who live in certain places

rain forest—a thick, green forest that receives a lot of rain

tropical—relating to a warm place near the equator

wetland—an area of land that is covered with low levels of water for most of the year

To Learn More

AT THE LIBRARY

Clarke, Ginjer L. *Life in the Amazon Rainforest*. New York, N.Y.: Penguin Random House, 2018.

Hansen, Grace. *Brazil*. Minneapolis, Minn.: Abdo Kids, 2020.

Vilela, Fernando. *Along the Tapajós*. Translated by Daniel Hahn. New York, N.Y.: Amazon Crossing Kids, 2019.

ON THE WEB

FACTSURFER

Factsurfer.com gives you a safe, fun way to find more information.

1. Go to www.factsurfer.com.
2. Enter "Brazil" into the search box and click 🔍.
3. Select your book cover to see a list of related content.

Index

Amazon Rain Forest, 6
Amazon River, 6, 7, 11
animals, 10, 11
Brasília, 4, 5
Brazil facts, 20-21
Brazilian Highlands, 8, 11
capital (see Brasília)
Carnaval, 18, 19
Catholics, 12
cities, 5, 12
families, 14
foods, 16, 17
grasslands, 8
Independence Day, 19
Lent, 18
map, 5
Pantanal, 9, 10

people, 12, 16, 18, 19
picnics, 14
Portuguese, 12, 13
São Paulo, 12
say hello, 13
size, 4
soccer, 15
South America, 4
volleyball, 15
wetland, 9

The images in this book are reproduced through the courtesy of: lazyllama, front cover; Gustavo Frazao, front cover; rocharibeiro, pp. 2-3; outsideclick, p. 3; Erich Sacco, pp. 4-5; SL-Photography, p. 6; mantaphoto, pp. 6-7; Angela_Macario, pp. 8-9; Hakat, p. 9; buteo, pp. 10-11; imageBroker/ Alamy, p. 11 (hyacinth macaw); Giedriius, p. 11 (caiman); COULANGES, p. 11 (Amazon river dolphin); Pascale Gueret, p. 11 (giant anteater); filipfrazao, p. 12; Brastock, pp. 12-13; Siker Stock, pp. 14-15; A.RICARDO, p. 15 (soccer, inset); RHJPhotos, p. 16 (freioada); Davi Correa, p. 16 (quindim); Anderson Stange, p. 16 (brigadeiros); Joa Souza, p. 17; Celso Pupo, pp. 18-19; titoOnz, p. 20 (flag); Alizada Studios, p. 20 (Neymar da Silva Santos Júnior); Juan Camilo Bernal, p. 21 (Christ the Redeemer); Nido Huebl, p. 21 (Iguaçu Falls); Catarina Belova, p. 21 (Sugar Loaf Mountain); ckchiu, pp. 22-23.